Live Debt Free – Change your Life

Live Debt Free – Change your Life

Copyright © All Rights Reserved

About the Book

The objective of this book to showcase a roadmap to achieve Financial Freedom using real-life examples. Even though, I had worked with major corporations, I felt financially inadequate and always stressed about the future. I was always wondering,

How to achieve Financial Freedom and start working less and stressing less about the future while living every moment of my life?

I had seen my parents, relatives and neighbours going about the traditional way of getting an education, securing a job for life, savings in banks, investing in stocks & shares, retiring on pensions some for the better and rest for the worse and some relying heavily on their children for support during their grey years.

Traditionally, options for financial planning meant,

- Savings in banks
- Pensions Plans
- Stock market portfolio
- Business investment
- Property portfolio

Most of the people planned their financial future based on the first two options i.e., savings in banks and pension plans. The more adventurous ventured into stocks & shares, invested in business or property.

But, there has been a paradigm shift as we moved from an Industrial Age to the Information and Digital Age. The Industrial Age was characterised with guaranteed life time jobs and assured pensions while the life-span of a person was shorter than today. However, the Information and Digital Age has made our jobs less secure and short-lived while the life span of a person has become longer.

Today, the first three options have all become less appealing and incapable of securing a secure financial future. The savings rates in banks have dwindled to an all-time low or nil, pension plans have gone bust and the stocks have hardly rallied since the tech bubble except for a few blue chip companies provided you were lucky to have been an insider with access at the IPO stage. You cannot get a decent return from bank savings plans, stocks are volatile, government backed pensions and investments aren't as secure as they used to be and people have lost faith. Investing in business is an expensive and risky proposition and not many have the courage nor appetite to start and remain for the long run.

It is in this context that only property seems to be a relatively secure option and has consistently performed well against inflation provided you have not been over ambitious. But the first steps towards achieving it is by starting to save and reducing your debts.

This book will show you how to move up the ladder right from

- how to start saving,
- how to clear your debt,

Author	Roco
Copyright & Published by	infage
Version	1.00
Dated	2015

Live Debt Free – Change your Life

Limits of Liability & Disclaimer of Warranty

The author and publisher of this book and the associated materials have used their best efforts in preparing this material. The author and publisher make no representations or warranties with respect to the accuracy, applicability, fitness, or completeness of the contents of this material. They disclaim any warranties expressed or implied, merchantability, or fitness for any particular purpose. The author and publisher shall in no event be held liable for any loss or other damages, including but not limited to special, incidental, consequential, or other damages. If you have any doubts about anything, the advice of a competent professional should be sought. The names of any software mentioned in this book are trademarks of their respective software providers and for the benefit of such companies with no intention of infringement of the trademark. Any unauthorised reprint or use of this material is prohibited.

About the Author

Roco, is a Management and Financial Consultant by profession. I have worked for many of the top consultancies and blue chip companies for nearly two decades and learnt that a job does not always guarantee financial security for me or my family.

Being on moderate income, but spending on the niceties of life during the peak years of our lives meant that we were slogging day in and day out and looking forward to a rather bleak future. The more we earned, the more we spent thanks to inflation, increased demands of a growing family and other commitments. At the end of the day, we felt we had very little left.

There were occasions when we were virtually bankrupt during three different stages of our lives. If this was the stage we were in during our peak years, we were dreading to think of our days as we aged. Amidst all the travel, salaries, bonuses, pensions and high life, it was obvious that we couldn't rely on pensions alone and we had to have a Plan B – *"Be your own Boss to secure Financial Freedom"*.

There must be something more out there that successful people who have achieved Financial Freedom do and are good at doing it in a better way. And, I wanted to know their secret - The secret to Financial Freedom.

The best way to find out was just trying the different strategies and techniques that the successful people put in practice. This book will show you everything that they went through, so you too can learn from their trials and tribulations and achieve Financial Freedom and enjoy your life now and in the future.

Contents

About the Book 3

About the Author 7

What is Financial Freedom? 11

When do you achieve Financial Freedom? 17

What are the key drivers of Financial Freedom? 23

How can you achieve Financial Freedom? 27

First Basic Steps towards Financial Freedom 32

Step 1: How to start Saving? 33

    Triple Pay Rule 36

    50 minus Age Formula 41

Step 2: How to be debt free? 43

    Two types of Debts: 45

        Good Debt: 46

        Bad Debt: 53

    What is Bad Debt Repayment Plan? 60

    Two methods of Bad Debt Repayment Plan 61

        First Pay High Interest Debt 61

        Self-Debt Consolidation 69

Conclusion 73

Live Debt Free – Change your Life

What is Financial Freedom?

Most of us are herded like sheep to live a stereotypical life from a young age starting with 10-18 years of education, followed by the prospect of a permanent job, and continue working for 40 odd years until retirement or death. It was a classical life cycle during the Industrial Age.

SECRET: Working like a dog for decades is out. Financial Freedom is in.

But, the Industrial Age has long since gone and we have moved to the Information and Digital Age where jobs are no longer permanent, the lifespan has increased and university degrees don't really matter unless you are heading to be a professional like a doctor, scientist, professor, teacher, nurse, to name a few.

SECRET: *Industrial Age has made way to the Information and Digital Age and we need to evolve accordingly.*

Today, permanent jobs seem to be a thing of the past, graduates are entering the workforce carrying huge university fee debts even before they get their first pay cheque, savings interest is very low, stocks are stagnant and getting on the property ladder seems virtually impossible.

Hence, there is a real big problem in applying what worked in the Industrial Age to the Information and Digital Age. We cannot follow the same old linear path of our parents and grand-parents from primary school to death. We may not have the luxury of spending majority of our lives at work, trying to climb the corporate ladder, get a salary raise, buy a bigger house, fill it with comfort that may not be necessary. We may be able to have the freedom to make life decisions or travel the world or spend time with our family and children only after we retire. Right?

Well, not for me. I can't speak for you or anyone else, but I find that life scenario boring and repulsive. I always thought that I would retire in my forties and pursue what I like most. In the interim, I would like to have the ability to change careers, work in different countries across different time-zones, take some time off, or pursue whatever I wanted during my free time. What was of paramount importance was not what I chose to do, but the very thought of having the freedom to choose and reinvent my life at different stages of my lifecycle.

FINANCIAL FREEDOM

IS NOT	IS
Winning a lottery or a windfall	Living every moment of your life
Having money but no health	Having passive income to meet living expenses
Having money but no time	Having health and time to enjoy your passive income
Being stuck in a rat race	A learning journey

The fundamental aspect I am raising is of Financial Freedom.

- Do I have the ability to make life decisions without worrying about tomorrow?

- Am I in a position to quit my job without worrying about my next pay cheque?

Are we living a Life of debt or a Life of hand to mouth or a Life of wealth? In a life of debt, we are constantly living on credit by borrowing from people, banks and institutions. A lot of people are in this boat constantly struggling in a debt cycle especially during times of recession. In a life of hand to mouth, we are constantly striving to live from pay cheque to pay cheque. A lot of salaried people are in this boat struggling to balance the books. In a life of wealth, we generate more income than our expenses. Very few of us are in this boat and generally own business or smart investors.

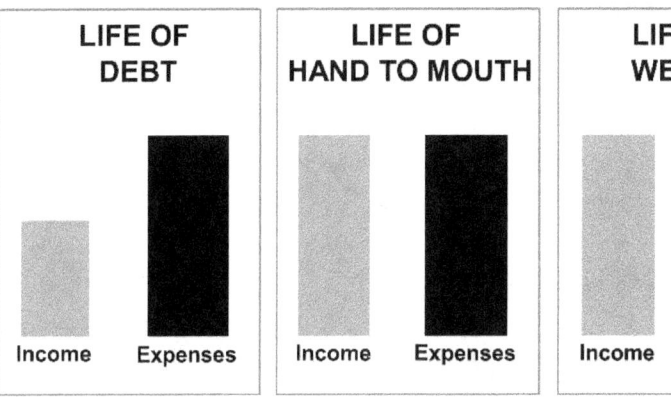

Financial freedom is the stage at which you feel financially independent or able to have an early retirement even if it means for a short time to pursue your "*Life's Calling or Purpose*". If you don't have a purpose in life, please do not retire as I have seen enough people lost after retirement, losing the meaning of life and sometimes even dying out of boredom. Their life was synonymous with work even though they had saved enough for retirement.

Financial Freedom is much more than having enough money. It is the freedom to be who you really are and do what you really want in life. To achieve Financial Freedom, you need to transform into a different person than you are today and let go of whatever that has held you back. It is a spiritual and emotional journey to become a happy and successful person in achieving your *Life's Calling or Purpose*. This is the true revelation of Financial Freedom.

SECRET: Financial Freedom is the ability to make life style changing decisions.

It doesn't necessarily require you to stop working and abandoning your family and commitments. It is about making your life and that of your family better. Money can come and go at any time but Time lost can never return. However, having sufficient money gives you the freedom to spend your time as you see fit.

SECRET: Money does not make you Rich. Time and not Money is your most valuable asset.

Ask Yourself these Questions,

- How would I spend my remaining years if money weren't an issue?

- Do I live my life fully and do I love my life well?

When do you achieve Financial Freedom?

Financial freedom is the point in your life when your portfolio of assets like fixed deposits, ISAs, stocks, bonds, property investments, etc. can produce enough passive income to cover your baseline expenses. The passive income is generally in the form of dividends, interest, rentals from properties and capital appreciation. In other words, you no longer need to work and get an active income or salary to pay for your daily living expenses.

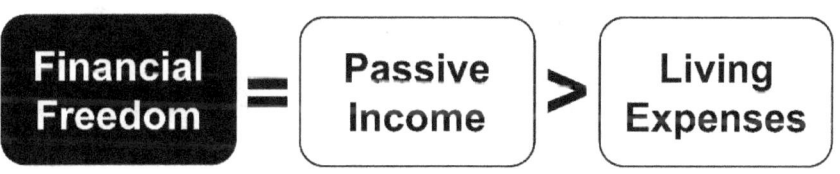

Assets and liabilities are critical factors in determining if you have achieved Financial Freedom. An asset is anything of value that can be liquidated if you have a debt. A liability is related to debt and it your responsibility to compensate for it. For example, a house is your asset and the mortgage on it is your liability. Similarly, a rental property is an asset for the landlord and a car is a liability. An asset increases in value where as a liability decreases in value over a period of time.

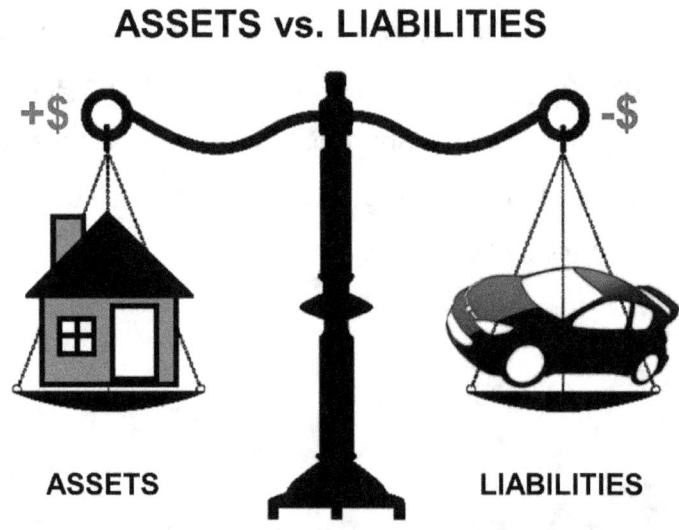

Generally, you can withdraw 5% (assuming it is the inflation rate) of your portfolio each year without reducing the capital in your assets.

SECRET: An asset increases in value where as a liability decreases in value over a period of time.

If you are 25 years old and your expenses are only £1000 per month and you have assets that generate £1000 or more per month, then you have achieved Financial Freedom and have the freedom to pursue your *Life's Calling or Purpose* without worrying about money. The chances of this happening are rare unless you have a huge family inheritance or won a lottery or a windfall or made a significant invention that was commercially successful.

If on the other hand, you are 50 years old and earn a £200,000 per year but still have expenses above £200,000 a year, then you have not achieved Financial Freedom because you still have to generate the difference to stay even. Hence, you may not have the luxury to pursue your *Life's Calling or Purpose*.

SECRET: Age is irrelevant to achieve Financial Freedom.

It does not matter how old or young someone is or how much money they have or make. If they can generate enough money to meet their needs from passive income other than their main job, then they have achieved Financial Freedom.

Financial Freedom is relative to your status and also your lifestyle. If you are single with a simple lifestyle, the chances are that your assets required to generate a passive income is lower and achievable earlier.

Peter was 30 years old, single and his living expenses was about £10,000 a year. He would need a portfolio of assets of about £200,000 which at the rate of 5% generates £10,000 a year. However, his passive income of £10,000 per year may not be enough for next year due to the effects of inflation. At 5% inflation, the living expenses would rise to £10,500 next year and $11,025 in the following year to maintain the same lifestyle. Hence, there will be a time when he would lose Financial Freedom because of inflation.

To achieve a passive income that is equal to or more than the inflation rate, you need to have a portfolio of assets which generates passive income equal to or more than the inflation rate. In other words, the gains from your assets needs to be equal to or more than 5% (assuming it is the inflation rate) every year.

Live Debt Free – Change your Life

In our first year of marriage, we spent £18,000 a year in Singapore. To secure our Financial Freedom, we would have to multiply our annual expenses by 20 for a 5% withdrawal (equals inflation rate). In other words, 1/0.05 = 20x, where x is the amount of annual expenses. This means we would need £360,000 (or 20 x 18,000) in our portfolio of assets. Realistically, we could live comfortably if we chose an area with lower cost of living. But, this gives a starting target to achieve our Financial Freedom.

Life is full of uncertainties and our Financial Freedom target may change if we decided to have children or if our health status changed. We have two young children and our annual expenses works out to be about £30,000. Taking this into account, our current Financial Freedom target is to accumulate approximately £600,000 (or 20 x 30,000) in our portfolio of assets based on 5% inflation. This portfolio must be able to sustain us even if the inflation rises.

We have seen many celebrities who have made millions of dollars and lost it all due to poor financial planning or life's choices. Most went bankrupt since their expenses were more than their income or because of divorce or because of lawsuits or foreclosures due to high levels of debt. They were financially wealthy but not financially free.

You have achieved Financial Freedom when your assets generate income more than your daily living expenses. However, just because you have money does not mean you have Financial Freedom.

What are the key drivers of Financial Freedom?

The key drivers of Financial Freedom are

- Secure retirement and
- Comfortable lifestyle

The reality is that most people fear that traditional ways of working and saving won't provide for a secure retirement or a comfortable lifestyle. People will have to work beyond retirement to sustain themselves or rely on their children or on charity if available.

Comfortable lifestyle doesn't necessarily mean flamboyant toys and greed. Most people have modest expectations when it comes to comfortable lifestyle.

A close friend of mine, Steve used to spend 1 hour 30 minutes per day commuting by train from home to work in Central London and another 1 hour 30 minutes commuting back from work to home. On a bad day, the commute would be more than 3 hours a day depending on train breakdowns, delays, traffic, overcrowding etc. He would start his commute at 7 am and reach home at 7 pm on a good day. This would mean he would miss the school runs in the morning and evening to drop and pick up his kids from school; he would be too exhausted to play with them in the evening; sometimes he would reach home after they had slept in the night and had hardly any time to spend with his wife Sally. Sally had her own routine working locally while managing the kids' school runs, homework and taking care of them. Both Steve and Sally were doing this Monday to Friday, 5 days a week. The only days they were relatively free were Saturday and Sunday. But, even the weekends were filled with swimming and music lessons for the kids.

All that Steve and Sally were hoping was for a better lifestyle wherein they had enough time to spend with their kids and each other.

Does this lifestyle and expectation sound familiar?

Steve and Sally were tired of this lifestyle since it was having a toll on their relationship and on their kids. They had to either live with it or have a better quality of life by making some hard choices that would lead to a better life for them and their children.

Steve had a choice to either search for a job closer to home which may pay lesser or try working flexible hours at a lower pay and have a better quality of life. Due to the difficult job market, he decided to talk to his boss and work out flexible working arrangements wherein he would work 3 days in office and 2 days from home at a reduced pay. Steve and his family's quality of life increased remarkably.

It is evident from the above example, that the key driver is the urge for a better quality of life and a comfortable lifestyle. The expectations change as you age and could become lesser as you near retirement. Most people have modest expectations for a comfortable lifestyle. Some of them include:

- Spending more time with family
- Working flexible working hours
- Less commute to and from work
- Nice holiday in a year
- Affordable babysitters for timeouts
- House cleaner
- Good dinner in a restaurant
- Shopping for clothes or gadgets
- Spa package once in a while

You can probably think of many more.

The bottom-line is, while some may be driven by luxury items, it is the little things in life that actually improve the quality of life leading to a comfortable living.

How can you achieve Financial Freedom?

We know that Financial Freedom is driven by the urge to life a comfortable life and have a secure retirement. You don't require a huge portfolio of assets to generate a passive income to compliment or supplement your regular income. You have different ways of achieving this objective like savings plans, stocks & shares, pensions, investments in business and property.

As discussed earlier, the first three options have had a lacklustre performance in the hands of so called expert fund managers or they need an enormous amount of focus and time on a daily basis to manage it ourselves. This leaves us with the last two options. Investing in a business is risky and you need to be an expert in the field of business you are investing to safeguard your limited capital.

My preferred choice is a property portfolio to achieve a better quality of lifestyle and a secure retirement. The primary reason for my preferred choice is because of the *Power of Leveraging*.

For example, if you put £5,000 in an ISA (savings plan), you need to put the full amount; if you buy £5,000 worth of shares, you need to pay £5,000; if you put £5,000 into a new business, again you need to put in the whole amount although you could take a business loan; if you put £5,000 in a pension plan, your employer and the government may top it up, but government will take it back in the form of tax on your annuity and you are not allowed to withdraw it fully on retirement. None of these options have the option of leveraging.

The chart below shows the performance of £10,000 invested between 1996 and 2016 across different investment instruments.

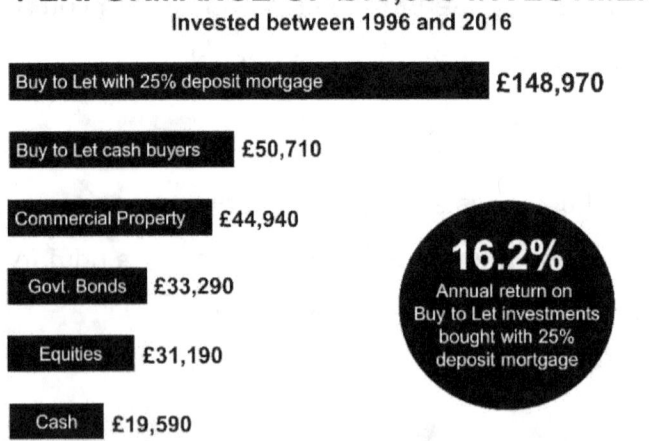

The power of leveraging can be best explained through an example.

George was a graduate trainee who worked with me in an organisation as an intern during his University days. A few years later, he bought a new-build 1 bed apartment worth £150,000 using only £10,000 as deposit. The builder paid the remaining deposit of £12,500 and also absorbed the 1% stamp duty fees.

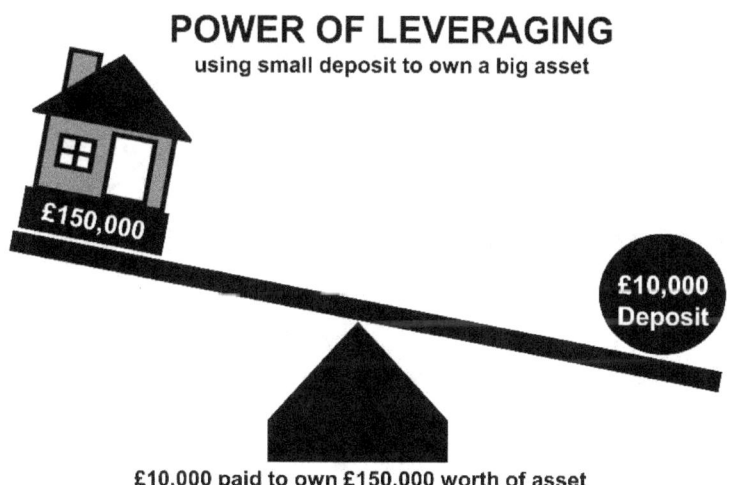

£10,000 paid to own £150,000 worth of asset

The rest of the amount of £127,000 was lent using 85% mortgage from a bank on a 2 year fixed interest rate of 2.9%. George owned an asset worth £150,000 with only a £10,000 of his own money.

We can see the power of leveraging in the above example. George being single was not only a proud owner of his house but also was on the property ladder with just £10,000. In two years, the apartment had appreciated to £175,000. George had a choice to either remortgage and release the equity or sell the apartment.

If he decided to sell the apartment, the mortgage lending bank would only want the loaned amount back leaving the profit with George. George would have been left with approximately £25,000 profit even after repaying his mortgage. For simplicity, this doesn't take into account the mortgage interest paid in the two years or other capital gains that may be applicable.

SECRET: Successful investment is all about leveraging, and only property investment has that beautiful edge.

Obviously, you don't achieve Financial Freedom with just one property. But the above example highlights the *Power of Leveraging* that can be used repeatedly to reach that goal. It is not always a necessity to own a huge property portfolio to achieve Financial Freedom. The size of the portfolio depends on the lifestyle you want and the amount it costs. The passive income generated by your property portfolio should be more than your lifestyle expenses.

SECRET: Passive income generated by your property portfolio should exceed your expenses.

First Basic Steps towards Financial Freedom

Financial Freedom is achieved when your assets generate income more than your daily living expenses. Financial Freedom is much more than having enough money. It is the freedom to be who you really are and do what you really want in life.

It is great to know that we all aspire to be Financially Free. But, how do we achieve this financial goal.

Based on life experiences of the financially independent, there are two basic steps towards achieving Financial Freedom. They are,

    Step 1: Start Saving

    Step 2: Reduce debt

We will start exploring each of these steps in detail in the subsequent chapters.

Step 1: How to start Saving?

Saving is one of the basic steps towards Financial Freedom. You can save for a holiday, for a course, for university, for a wedding or for a house. Property is the most promising and safer investment which involves minimal effort and minimal investment thanks to the Power of Leveraging. The minimal investment refers to the deposit paid on a house. Regular savings will result in accumulation of deposit for your first house.

There are various instruments to start the habit of saving. Most banks provide such saving instruments like Regular Savings Plan, Fixed Deposits and Investment Savings Account (ISA). While interest paid on savings accounts are taxable, ISAs provide tax free interest. There is a limit on the amount you can save in an ISA and it varies each year.

Most of us struggle to start and stick to our regular savings plan. We start a New Year with a resolution to save and give up half way through the year and land up with no savings or in debt. It is mainly attributed to a common reason, "We just don't have anything left by the end of the month due to the high cost of living". This is the predicament faced by a variety of people starting from those earning £1,000 to £10,000 per month.

When I used to live in Singapore, I was introduced to the concept of saving by a government enforced compulsory savings program called the Central Provident Fund (CPF). In those days, 20% of my salary was paid into my CPF account and it was topped up by an equal amount by my employer. Assuming my salary of S$1000 per month, this would work out to be S$400 per month in my CPF account with S$200 deducted from my salary and S$200 contributed by my employer. This amount deposited into my CPF account could not be withdrawn by me. It could only be used to fund three important aspects of life,

- **Housing** – *deposit and mortgage payments each month to buy my first apartment*
- **Healthcare** - *health insurance premiums to meet medical emergencies such as surgery or pregnancy*
- **Retirement** - *investments in Stocks and Shares*

The remaining 80% of my salary could be used anyway I wanted after deducting taxes. The beauty of this program was that at the end a year, I could see a substantial amount of savings in my CPF account that I could use for the three important aspects of my life mentioned above. Whatever remained in the CPF account over the years would form my pension pot when I retired.

A similar concept exists in other countries too either as a provident fund or pensions or 401(k) plans.

Triple Pay Rule

The Singapore program of deducting 20% of my salary each month into my CPF account taught me the concept of paying myself first before spending on anything else. I extended this concept further and came up with a *Triple Pay Rule*,

- *Pay myself first*
- *Pay my debts and finally*
- *Pay my expenses*

As I learnt from the Singapore CPF Program, Pay myself First covered,

- Housing
- Healthcare and
- Retirement

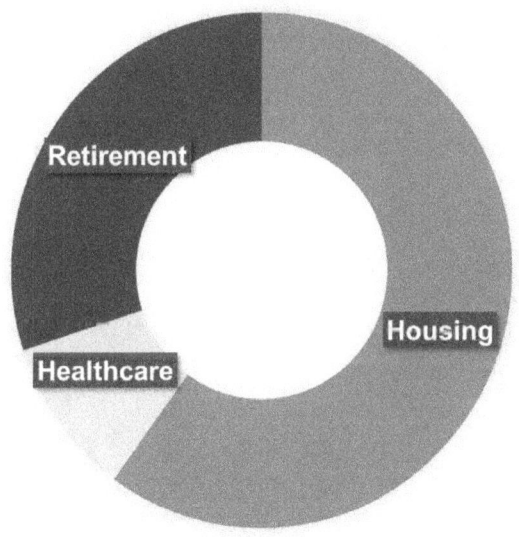

How much you pay yourself, your debts and your expenses is subjective and depends on your location, your lifestyle and your end goal. Some use 10% to pay themselves first where as others pay as much as 20% to 30%. You can start with a modest 10% first until you have firmly established it as a habit and then increase it to 20% or more. Obviously, the remaining 80% should allow you to live a decent lifestyle. It is generally advisable to save a higher percentage of your net income after taxes during your younger days as the commitments normally increase as you grow older and have a family.

Peter was a graduate trainee and was on a first job paying £13,000 gross per year. After deducting all taxes, he used to get 1,000 per month in net salary. He started using the **Triple Pay Rule** *and split his net salary each month as*

- **30% - Pay myself First**:
  £300 was paid into a savings plan such as ISA and left untouched

- **10% - Pay my Debts**:
  £100 was used to pay off his student loans and other debts

- **60% - Pay my Expenses**:
  £600 was left for his monthly expenses including rent, transportation, food and entertainment

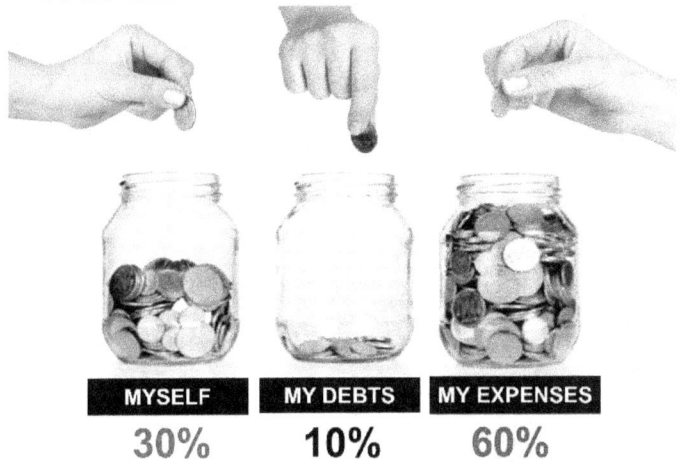

At the end of the first year, he had £3.600 in savings and within 2 years he had £7,200. Hence, Peter adopted the 30:10:60 rule to split his net income.

The most important lesson we learn from Peter, is how we can start early the habit of saving and how we could allocate a higher percentage of our net income as savings while we are still single with less commitments. Believe me, it will become increasingly difficult to save more than 30% as you start having a family and additional commitments. Hence, it is advisable to start with a higher allocation for savings as a percentage of your net income when you are younger.

Conversely, as you age your regular job income will be higher than your income when you just started working first. Although, the percentage allocated may drop as you age due to other family commitments, the amount allocated for savings may be more than your when you first started saving.

For example, if you have a monthly net income after taxes of £1,000 when you first started working in your twenties, your allocation to Pay myself First may be 30% which works out to £300 per month. However, when you are in your forties, if your net monthly salary after taxes is £4,000, then your allocation to Pay myself First may be 10% which works out to £400 per month. The percentage allocated for savings has dropped from 30% in your twenties to 10% in your forties but the monthly amount saved has increased from £300 in your twenties to £400 in your forties.

SECRET: Triple Pay Rule caters to first paying yourself, then your debts and finally your expenses.

50 minus Age Formula

The *50 minus Age Formula* is a formula that I arrived at based on my experiences and the challenges in saving at different stages of my life. To keep it simple, I started using a formula based on my age to determine the percentage allocated to Pay myself First.

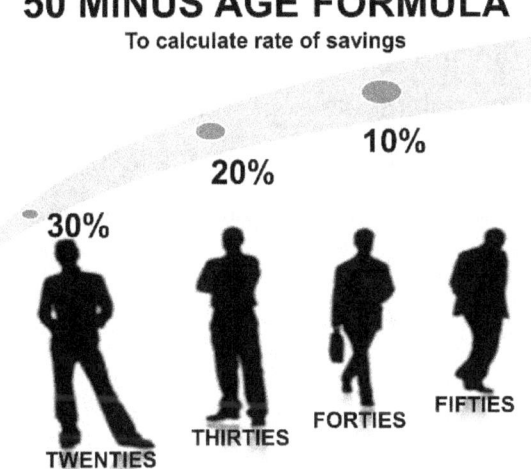

The *50 minus Age Formula* can be best explained as, if you are in your

- **Twenties**, you could start by saving **30%** (50 – 20) of your net income

- **Thirties**, you could save **20%** (50 – 30) of your net income

- **Forties**, you could save **10%** (50 – 40) of your net income

- **Fifties and above**, you have passive income to supplement your main income.

If you are in your fifties and your passive income is no way close to your regular job income, please do not panic. If your passive income doesn't supplement your regular job income then hopefully, it complements your main income so that you can work less hours and have a better quality of life. This rule is not set in stone and it is up to you to save what you can for your retirement and to suit your lifestyle.

SECRET: The concepts of "Pay myself First" and the "50 minus Age Formula" will help you land on the First Step towards Financial Freedom.

Step 2: How to be debt free?

Debt is money borrowed from another person or institution to pay for your lifestyle. It is essentially *Other People's Money*. Debt is inevitable. At some stage, we have seen our parent's or ourselves taking loans to meet emergencies.

Some of us are so addicted to credit cards and store cards and use it to shop, sometimes living beyond our means. The shopping ranges from high range items such as homes, cars and branded clothing to daily items such as vehicle fuel, groceries and chocolates. It is no wonder that a lot of people in our society live on borrowed money which just keeps accumulating both in terms of principal and interest on the principal amount.

The same trend manifests itself at the national level leading to many nations in severe debt since their expenditure is more than their Gross Domestic Product (GDP), which is the income a country generates. It is no wonder that today we have more countries in debt than anytime in previous generations. Although debt sounds bad, not all of the debts are bad; some are good too.

In this chapter, we will learn how to reduce debt and prevent being skint or broke all the time. But before we learn to be debt free, we need to understand the different types of debt and how they impact us in our daily lives.

Two types of Debts:

There are two types of debt. They are,

- Good Debt
- Bad Debt

Do you have Good Debt or Bad Debt?

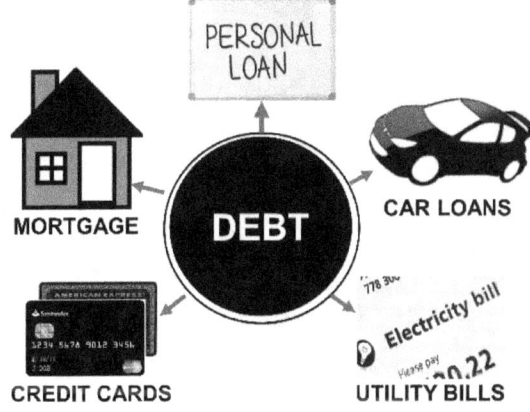

Good Debt:

Good debt is used to generate passive income which is greater than the interest rate on the loan taken. Good debt increases your net financial value which is also referred to as Net Worth.

Examples of good debt include investments in real estate, starting your own business and earning your own education.

Real Estate:

 It is one of the biggest investment made using good debt called mortgage. We buy our house using a small deposit and pay the balance using a mortgage by borrowing the rest from a bank or housing society. In a previous example, I mentioned about George.

George bought a new-build 1 bed apartment worth £150,000 using only £10,000 as deposit. The builder paid the remaining deposit of £12,500 and also absorbed the 1% stamp duty fees. The rest of the amount of £127,500 was lent using an 85% mortgage from a bank on a two year fixed interest rate of

2.9%. George owned an asset worth £150,000 with only a £10,000 of his own money.

In the above example, £127,500 is the good debt that was used to buy an asset worth £150,000. In two years, the apartment had appreciated to £175,000. George had a choice to either remortgage and release the equity or sell the apartment. If he decided to sell the apartment, the mortgage lender would only want the loaned amount plus interest back leaving the profit with George. George would have been left with approximately £25,000 profit even after repaying his mortgage. George put down only £10,000 of his own money and used £127,500 of Other People's Money as Good Debt to generate a profit of approximately £25,000 in 2 years. For simplicity, this doesn't take into account the mortgage interest paid in the two years or other capital gains tax that may be applicable.

Own Business:

Many of us are driven by the prospect of being our own boss and working for ourselves either as a sole trader or through a limited company or partnership by joining hands with others. In all these three types of entrepreneurs, we invest a small amount of our own money and borrow *Other People's Money* in the form of Good Debt with the sole intention of making more money out of money. The prospect of hiring yourself, working for yourself and paying yourself and others is a major attraction. You can realise your dream by using Good Debt to start a business and grow it into a public limited company by borrowing more Good Debt in the form of Initial Public Offering (IPO) resulting in a huge wealth and a mammoth public company.

A close associate of mine, Richard started a digital media business selling songs, movies and games online using £25,000 of his own money. Due to the initial success of his business and to meet an increased demand with estimated revenue of £500,000 per year he had to raise additional capital of £100,000 to expand his business. He secured a loan from his bank using his business as collateral. This loan of £100,000 was a Good Debt which would be used to generate more revenues and profit.

After two years, his revenues grew to more than £1,000,000 a year yielding a net profit after taxes of £100,000 a year. Richard used only £25,000 of his own money and £100,000 of

Other People's Money to generate a revenue of more than £1,000,000 and a net profit after taxes of £100,000. In other words, he was able to make a profit out of the Good Debt that enriched him by £100,000 in net profit.

In today's Information and Digital Age, there are more people venturing into entrepreneurship to build their own business using other people's money and time.

Own Education:

It is common knowledge that education is a visa to higher wages and jobs especially white collar jobs. Education has played a pivotal role to develop white collar professionals such as doctors, engineers, solicitors, financial experts, nurses or technical experts such plumbers, electricians etc. The chances of getting a good paying job rises with proper education, qualifications and certifications.

Today, most of the investment in higher education is borne by students themselves through a loan. However, there may be exceptions where in parent's bear the costs of higher education of their children. Either way, there is a lifetime investment made with the hope that the benefits will be reaped by the children after their education through good paying jobs or self-employment. Hence, there is a return on investment over a lifetime to enable an educated person to build a successful portfolio and a comfortable lifestyle.

Ed was a student who studied medicine in a UK Medical School using a loan to pay for tuition fees of £9000 per year. Being a bright student, he was successful to get scholarship. By the time he completed his degree and was ready to practice he had a sizable student loan running into thousands. He was hired by the National Health Service (NHS) and he was able to start clearing his debt slowly.

In this scenario, the educational loan was a good debt that helped him get into a profession of his choice and also serve the society.

Todays, most graduates are carrying huge amounts of student loan debt when they graduate out of university. Too many people doing the same degrees may result in excess supply of resources for few roles in demand in a particular area. This becomes acute during times of recession and depression. Some of the graduates are struggling to find suitable graduate entry level jobs due to the stagnant global economy while others have managed to start a business of their own. Hence, it is important to make a judicious choice of a career depending on your actual ambition in life. Education doesn't always guarantee a secure income or a permanent job.

Some people also borrow to invest in stocks, shares, commodities, precious metals, futures and foreign exchange. However, all these investment choices are subject to market risks and the so called good debt taken may turn out to be bad debt if they have no returns or if they result in loss of investments. We do not advise taking loans to invest in short term investments like stocks and shares whether it is done by yourself or through a fund manager as they are volatile and need daily monitoring.

The same risks hold good for real estate or for starting your own business or in investing in your own education. Sometimes the good debt taken to achieve them may turn out to be bad debt if due diligence is not taken. Sometimes, greed takes over and we soak ourselves in too much of debt with the hope of making a killing in investment returns only to find it fall like a house of cards.

Classic examples of such instances includes a serial real estate portfolio which is based on a series of mortgages leveraging on preceding properties with minimal capital. During a recession, normally the house prices and rental incomes fall while the mortgage rates, taxes, maintenance and service costs increase or remain the same thereby reducing your net gain and equity in your portfolio.

Similarly, a risky business venture without a good business plan or expertise is subject to risks and market fluctuations that may result in costing more than the investment thereby giving negative returns.

SECRET: Fortunes can be made with debt. They could also be lost due to debt.

Bad Debt:

Bad debt is mostly loans taken to finance your extravagant lifestyle beyond your means. These loans do not generate any passive income nor appreciate in value. On the contrary, they cost the person a lot in terms of repayment of both principal and interest. Missing one payment could attract penalties and more interest. Bad debt is any loan taken on depreciating assets which in turn decreases your Net Worth.

Examples of bad debt are purchase of extravagant clothing, gadgets, toys, holidays, services, cars, etc. paid using credit cards and store cards with exorbitant interest rates. These items do not appreciate nor generate any passive income. If used unintelligently and not paid back promptly, these bad debts could spiral out of control and rob off all your income each month.

It could land you in a never ending debt cycle where in you keep borrowing more and more to pay bad debts and mounting interest on it. A loan taken for a good intention like furnishing a house could turn into a bad debt if you fail to pay it back on time.

Credit Cards and Store Cards:

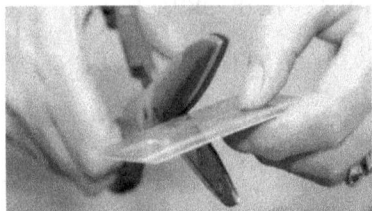

Credit cards and Store cards are the biggest culprits that put people in bad debt. Those plastic cards charge interest rates higher than personal loans and the payment cycles are scheduled to benefit the lenders.

It is always advisable to pay off the credit card in full even if used to buy daily usage items such as groceries and consumables. Never, should you miss a single minimal payment on your credit card since it not only attracts exorbitant daily/monthly interest rates and late payment fees but it also dents your personal credit score rating.

People with the worst bad debts generally have too many credit cards most of them maxed out to the full leading to a never ending cycle of debt. It is not a crime to possess two to three credit cards but the uncontrollable use of them is the cause of most miseries. If used intelligently, these credit cards could be valuable sources of liquidity to build assets which will be covered in later chapters.

Extravagant Clothing, Gadgets, Toys, Holidays, Services:

Most of the clothes, gadgets and toys lose half their value within a few weeks after purchase. Most of these items are bought using credit cards and any interest paid on it is an utter waste of your money; money that could have been used to generate assets of value. Similarly, extravagant holidays or vacations and personal services is money down the drain. It doesn't mean that you should not buy good clothes, gadgets, toys, holidays or services. It simply means buying them diligently and living within your means.

Cars:

Cars are expensive both to buy and maintain. New cars cost much more than used cars and they lose their value the moment you drive away from the showroom. We live in cities with inadequate or expensive public transport and the only choice is to own a car. A car enables you to drive to work, drop your children off to school and run errands in your life. However, hire purchase on a car involves paying a lot of interest leaving you with a depreciating asset and an inflating expense.

If you are on a tight income, it is wiser to buy a smaller and used car instead of a new and expensive car bought mainly to boost your ego and status in society. It normally makes more sense to pay off the hire purchase on a new or used car at the earliest or use a low interest personal loan to buy it. A car depreciates in value each year until it becomes worthless. Moreover, the operational costs such as fuel, insurance premiums, service, tax and any repairs make it all the more expensive for a car that depreciates each year until it becomes worthless.

Paul and Ruby were a hard working couple working as professional executives with good jobs. They owned a modest house and lived well within their means before they got into Executive Management positions. Since then, they loved to live the high life and owned a big house, expensive big car and club memberships; went on exclusive holidays and hosted flamboyant parties. In 2006, to maintain their status image in society, they bought an expensive large 5 bed room house in an exclusive and posh suburb in England at a cost of

£1,000,000; refurbished the full house at an expense of £100,000; bought 2 new exclusive executive and sports cars and went on exclusive holidays on business class flights each year. At the end of the first year they had a total debt of £1,000,000 with £800,000 in mortgage and the remaining £200,000 in bad debts spent on house furnishings, expensive cars and exclusive holidays. Within a year they had a child adding more costs to their daily lifestyle. They struggled to repay the bad debts in good times. When the economy turned sour due to the 2008 global financial crisis, they lost their jobs and were in a conundrum to make ends meet and repay these mounting bad debts.

The above example shows how normal people fall into bad debts due to excessive needs and egos to maintain their status in society. Unfortunately, the economy took a bad turn and they became victims of bad debts threatening their very lifestyle and survival.

There are other forms of bad debt such as debt consolidation loans, loans taken for investment and credit card reward programs. Debt consolidation firms play on the weakness of people straddled in numerous debts and offer schemes such as debt consolidation where all debts are consolidated into one loan with affordable repayments. Although it sounds good as one consolidated loan, the rates are normally higher or the repayments are much higher than what people can afford.

Similarly, borrowing money at a lower interest with a hope of earning a higher rate of interest through investments such as stocks, shares, futures and derivatives could prove risky and catastrophic for inexperienced investors.

Some credit card companies provide reward programs which offer free air miles, free cruises, cash back and other incentives to make you spend more using credit cards. Failure to pay these credit cards may cost you more interest repayments than the rewards you have been tempted with.

The reality is very few people can pay everything in cash or debit cards. We are increasingly living in a digital age with online shopping for consumables and services. The danger lies when we go overboard using credit cards since unlike cash we do not see an end until the limit on the card has reached. Many of us have fallen in bad debt trap and may have recovered from this habit. Some of us may be still in a bad debt trap and are looking for ways and means to get out of this cycle where we live each month from hand to mouth relying on credit cards and loans.

If you are one of them worried about bad debt and want to get out of this never ending cycle, then the *Bad Debt Repayment Plan* will help you reduce your debt and get a step closer to Financial Freedom.

What is Bad Debt Repayment Plan?

I had mentioned in the *First Step: How to start Saving?*, the concept of *Triple Pay Rule* which is,

- *Pay myself first*
- *Pay my debts and finally*
- *Pay my expenses*

Paying debt was the second important task of this rule. Here, our focus is on paying bad debts, the debts that have destroyed the lives of people who have been caught in a never ending cycle.

Two methods of Bad Debt Repayment Plan

The two methods in Bad Debt Repayment Plan are

- *First Pay High Interest Debt*: Paying the debt with the highest interest rate first while paying minimal payment on other debts.

- *Self-Debt Consolidation*: Consolidate all debts with high interests into a loan with low interest. This should not be mistaken with debt consolidation plans sold by debt consolidation lenders who have their own interests in mind.

First Pay High Interest Debt

Here, we focus on paying your debt with the highest interest rate first while making the minimal payments on the other debts. This concept is best explained using an example.

Edward and Maria, a hard working couple in their early thirties bought a three bed room house for themselves of value £500,000 with a mortgage of £425,000 and had additional loans of £120,000 using the maximum limit available on all their personal loans and credit cards. The total debt including mortgage and other loans is £545,000.

The £425,000 mortgage was used to buy a house that appreciates in value each year. Hence, it is good debt. The mortgage amount of £425,000 has the lowest interest rate of 2.90% with a monthly repayment of £1,500.

However, £120,000 debt was incurred to buy items that do not appreciate in value and it costs them more in interest. Hence it is referred to as bad debt.

Let us focus only on their bad debts of £120,000 and get to the bottom of it as highlighted in the table below. The debts are arranged in a descending order based on the rate of interest starting from the highest to the lowest.

#	Debt	Outstanding Balance	Rate of Interest	Monthly Minimum Repayment	Order of Payment
A	ABC Store Card	5000	27.90%	50	1
B	Car Hire Purchase	50000	23.00%	500	2
C	Lloyds Credit Card	10000	18.94%	100	3
D	HSBC Credit Card	10000	18.90%	100	4
E	Barclays Personal Loan	15000	4.90%	350	5
F	MBNA Credit Card (Balance Transfer)	5000	4.00%	50	6
G	Santander Personal Loan	10000	3.60%	100	7
H	Sainsbury Personal Loan	15000	3.40%	250	8
	TOTAL	120000		1500	

Live Debt Free – Change your Life

As displayed on the table, they have

   A. An ABC store card with an outstanding balance of £5,000 used to pay for clothing. It attracts the highest interest rate of 27.90% among all their debts. The monthly minimum repayment is £50.

   B. A Car Hire Purchase with an outstanding balance of 50,000 paid for 2 new cars. It attracts the second highest interest rate of 23% among all their debts. The monthly repayment is £500.

   C. A Lloyds Credit Card with maximum limit of £10,000 fully utilised to buy gadgets, holidays and furnishings. It attracts the third highest interest rate of 18.94% among all their debts. The monthly minimum repayment is £100.

   D. A HSBC Credit Card with maximum limit of £10,000 fully utilised to buy more consumables like clothes and services. It attracts the fourth highest interest rate of 18.90% among all their debts. The monthly minimum repayment is £100.

   E. A Barclays Personal Loan of £15,000 to build an extension to their house. It attracts the fifth highest interest rate of 4.90% among all their debts. The monthly minimum repayment is £350.

   F. A MBNA Credit Card that was used to transfer balance of £5,000 from other credit cards. It attracts the sixth highest interest rate of 4% among all their debts. The monthly minimum repayment is £50.

   G. A Santander Personal Loan of £10,000 to renovate their house. It attracts the seventh highest interest rate of 3.60% among all their debts. The monthly minimum repayment is £100.

H. A Sainsbury Personal Loan of £15,000 to extend their house and renovate it. It attracts the eighth highest interest rate of 3.40% among all their debts. The monthly minimum repayment is £250.

The total of all these bad debts is equal to £120,000 and the monthly minimum balance equals to £1,500.

Our objective is not only to reduce bad debt to zero but also to avoid paying interest rates as much as possible; the major cause of never ending cycle of bad debts. Hence, we need to start by first paying off debts that cost the highest interest rates. The table shows the bad debts arranged in descending order by interest rates. The column "Order of Payment" shows the order in which the bad debts need to be cleared while repaying the minimum amount on the rest of the bad debts.

Edward and Maria have a combined monthly net income of about £6,000. Using our **Triple Pay Rule**, they need to split their net income into

- **Pay myself first**
- **Pay my debts and finally**
- **Pay my expenses**

Pay myself first:

Since they are in their early thirties, using our 50 minus Age formula, they need to first pay 20% (50 – 30) of their net income to themselves. This works out to be about £1,200 per month (20% of £6,000) in savings.

Pay my debts:

As evident in the table, £1,500 of their net income goes to pay bad debts (excluding mortgage) each month. This works out to be 25% of their net income.

Pay my expenses:

The remaining £3,300 goes to pay for their expenses which includes the mortgage repayment of £1,500 each month. This works out to be 55% of their net income. This amount is sufficient to meet all their expenses each month.

*In the case of Edward and Maria, the Triple Pay formula was split as **20 : 25 : 55**,*

- ***20%** - Pay myself first*
  £1,200 was paid into an ISA or savings plan each month

- **25% - Pay my debts**
  £1,500 was used to pay off debts excluding mortgage each month

- **55% - Pay my expenses**
  £3,300 was used to pay for expense including mortgage each month

However, our objective is not only to reduce bad debt to zero but to avoid paying as much interest as possible. Using the *First Pay High Interest Debt*, they start making excess payments to the bad debt with the highest interest rate,

A. An ABC store card with an outstanding balance of £5,000 and the highest interest rate of 27.90% among all their debts. The monthly repayment increased from £50 to £600 per month by taking it out of the savings and they cleared this debt within a year.

Obviously, the Triple Pay formula will change as £600 out of the £1,200 savings will be used to pay the bad debt with the highest interest. The Triple Pay formula will change to **10 : 35 : 55**,

- **10% - Pay myself first**
- **35% - Pay my debts and finally**
- **55% - Pay my expenses**

The table above would change to:

#	Debt	Outstanding Balance	Rate of Interest	Monthly Minimum Repayment	Order of Payment
A	ABC Store Card	5000	27.90%	600	1
B	Car Hire Purchase	50000	23.00%	500	2
C	Lloyds Credit Card	10000	18.94%	100	3
D	HSBC Credit Card	10000	18.90%	100	4
E	Barclays Personal Loan	15000	4.90%	350	5
F	MBNA Credit Card (Balance Transfer)	5000	4.00%	50	6
G	Santander Personal Loan	10000	3.60%	100	7
H	Sainsbury Personal Loan	15000	3.40%	250	8
	TOTAL	**120000**		**2050**	

At the end of one year, Edward and Maria were able to clear bad debt A of £5,000 with the highest interest rate of 27.90% by over paying £600 per month instead of the minimum balance of £50. This practice saved them an unnecessary expense in accruing interest rates if they had prolonged the repayment period by just paying the minimum balance.

It is important to be disciplined not to use a credit card while you are still repaying it. When I asked them how they felt, they replied, "Very happy. We have our store card debt of £5,000 paid off fully and still have about £7,200 in our savings account since we paid ourselves first".

Once they cleared their bad debt A, they concentrated on the next big bad debt and keep repeating the above process. Using *First Pay High Interest Debt*, repeatedly, we can eliminate all bad debts one by one completely until we are debt free.

There is no hard and fast rule as far as the percentage breakdown in the *Triple Pay Rule* is concerned. It is adapted according to your situation. But it is important to use *Triple Pay Rule* to pay all three categories – yourself first, debt next and expenses last, to inculcate the discipline to achieve financial freedom.

Self-Debt Consolidation

It is another method that can be used to achieve Bad Debt Repayment Plan. Debt with higher interest rates are paid off using 0% balance transfers or 0% money transfers with a one off flat fee provided along with some credit cards. In some countries, they are also called Line of Credit and uses a cheque book.

Balance transfers are used to pay of your debts directly. Money transfers on the other hand, allows you to transfer money from the credit card into your bank account. It can they be used to pay off your debts with the highest interest rates.

In the previous example, once Edward and Maria cleared their bad debt A, they started concentrating on the next big bad debt B of £50,000 with the second highest interest rate of 23%. It was a car hire purchase loan taken for a duration of 10 years to purchase new cars. After one year, their outstanding balance was about £38,000. If they continued to pay £500 per month, they would continue to pay an interest of 23% per year on the outstanding balance. At the rate of 23% on a reducing balance this would work out to be £5,000 to 7,000 per year.

Since it is a car hire purchase, excess repayment is generally not allowed unless you make the full payment. But, Edward and Maria have the option to either use 0% balance transfers from cheaper credit cards charging only 3% flat fee and pay off the full balance or wait till the balance can be paid off fully using their savings.

Edward and Maria had a very good credit history since they never missed any payments on their debts. They were able to secure two credit cards with £20,000 limit each along with a 0% money transfer facility at a low rate of interest of only 3%. These two credit cards gave them the option to transfer about £40,000 into their bank accounts which was to be paid off in 2 years. They transferred 95% of their limits from their new credit cards into their bank account. This worked out to be £38,000 and paid a flat fee of 3% (£1,140) to the credit card company. The flat fee of £1,140 is much lesser than the interest of £5,000 to 7,000 per year they would have paid if they continued with the car hire purchase loan. Edward and Maria paid off the £38,000 balance on their car hire purchase loan using the money transferred into their bank accounts from the credit cards. They continued to pay the minimal monthly balance until it was time to pay off the full balance at the end of two years.

It is important to:

- Make only a maximum of 95% of the 0% balance/money transfer since the flat fee of 3% is taken off the credit card. In the case of Edward and Maria, it will work out to £38,000 + £1,140 flat fee = £39,140 which is lesser than the upper limit of £40,000. Else your balance/money transfer may be rejected or you will be charged the higher standard interest rate applied to credit cards which ranges between 18 to 23%.

- Lock these two new credit cards to avoid using them. Using them to purchase anything will nullify the 0% balance/money transfers and you will be subjected to the standard interest rate applied to credit cards which is 18 to 23%.

- Ensure minimal payments are made to all debts including these credit cards. Missing one payment will affect your Credit History for life and it will affect your credit rating throughout your life.

- Make sure you pay the outstanding balance within the end of two years.

SECRET: Huge savings can be achieved by moving bad debts with higher interest rates to a 0% credit card with balance or money transfer facility.

It is important to destroy all store cards and credit cards with high interest rates. It is sufficient to possess just one credit card for daily living expenses, while keeping one or two credit cards with cheap balance transfer facilities locked up to be used to create assets which will be discussed in subsequent chapters.

Conclusion

Life is all about choices. You made a choice to read this book since you wanted to achieve Financial Freedom by building a property portfolio. The reality is that most people fear that traditional ways of working and saving won't provide for a secure retirement or a comfortable lifestyle. People will have to work beyond retirement to sustain themselves or rely on their children or on charity if available. It is not always a necessity to own a huge property portfolio to achieve Financial Freedom. The size of the portfolio depends on the lifestyle you want and the amount it costs.

You have achieved Financial Freedom when your assets generate income more than your daily living expenses. However, just because you have money does not mean you have Financial Freedom. Financial freedom is the stage at which you feel financially independent or able to have an early retirement even if it means for a short time to pursue your "*Life's Calling or Purpose*".

The Triple Pay Rule and 50 Minus Age Formula are tools that will help you start saving and reduce your debts. Fortunes can be made with good debt. They could also be lost due to bad debt. These two tools along with the Power of Leveraging will help you start building your property portfolio.

This book may have opened your eyes to different possibilities. But, the proof is in the pudding and the actual transformation occurs when you have taken your first steps in saving and reducing debts. Life is a journey which will teach you that time is more precious than money. Time spent to follow your Life's Calling is more satisfying than being caught in the rat race of life making ends meet. Learning from every stage and experience of life is the biggest wealth. Start dreaming, never stop learning and continue achieving greater success.

Ultimately, the most valuable asset is the space you occupy in other people's heart. Wish you all the very best in your quest to build a property portfolio and achieve true Financial Freedom.

www.ingramcontent.com/pod-product-compliance
Lightning Source LLC
Chambersburg PA
CBHW050013230526
45470CB00003B/947